Common Law Marriage:

The Case for a Change in the Law

by
Jeremy Collingwood M.A. (Cantab.), B.D. (London)

Barrister-at-Law (Gray's Inn)
Vicar of Christ Church Guildford

GROVE BOOKS LIMITED
Bramcote Nottingham NG9 3DS

Contents

Page

Introduction...3
    – Why Another Booklet? 3
    – The Issue of Cohabitation...4
    – The Facts of Cohabitation...4

1.   The Biblical Evidence 7

2.   The Pastoral Approach 9

3.   The General Synod Debate 13

4.   A Brief Account of Marriage Law in England 15
    – The Legal Differences Between Cohabitation and Marriage.................17

5.   Should Common Law Marriage Status Be Granted to Cohabitants in
    Settled and Committed Relationships? 19

6.   Conclusions..23

7.   Proposals 24

First Impression April 1994.
ISSN 0951-2667
ISBN 1 85174 264 6

Introduction

Cohabitation is not a new problem, but it is a growing one and it stubbornly refuses to go away. For a long time, the Church of England has played Nelson and turned a blind eye to the subject, but now there are passionate voices exhorting the Church to do something about cohabitation. We are told, on the one hand, to stand up for Christian morality and no longer countenancé the marriage of those 'living in sin'. On the other hand, we are told that a cohabiting relationship can be as good as, and sometimes better than, a married one. General Synod has debated the issue and revealed an enormous range of pastoral attitudes to cohabitation. Recently I was phoned by a young woman, living in the parish, who asked if I would be willing to conduct her marriage with her boy friend. She said, 'Does it matter that we are living together?' She explained that another church had been willing to marry her fiancé and herself until it was discovered that they were living together. She said, 'I don't want you to marry us just because you have to. What is your attitude?' So the question stands, 'What is our attitude to cohabitation?' How should young people view it? What about parents? Should it make any difference to a marriage service in Church? Does the law on marriage need to be changed?

Why Another Booklet?

This is the third Grove Ethical Study on cohabitation. Greg Forster's *Marriage Before Marriage? The Moral Validity of 'Common Law' Marriage*, No. 69, which was first published in 1988, set the agenda. It was primarily a Christian sociological view of the growth in cohabitation. In 1992, Gary Jenkins's *Cohabitation; A Biblical Perspective*, No. 84, looked at cohabitation from a biblical viewpoint and sought to set out some pastoral guidelines. In 1991 Edward Pratt published privately his booklet, *Living in Sin?*[1] This argued that cohabitation offended against traditional Christian morality and should be condemned.

My booklet is a legal study of marriage and cohabitation in biblical and English history up to the present day. It seeks to build on the foundations laid by Greg Forster and Gary Jenkins to argue that the sociological changes in the nature of the family require buttressing by a legal framework in which common law marriage would acquire legal recognition in certain circumstances. It is submitted that, far from undermining Christian ethics as suggested by Edward Pratt, the legal recognition of common law marriage is a way of strengthening the family and securing the rights of the parties and their children. Failure to face up to the creeping marginalization of traditional marriage will not solve any of the practical and pastoral issues involved. I believe that the Church should be pro-active in seeking legislative changes which safeguard the Christian understanding of marriage, and not be forced to react to changes imposed by others. At the moment the law is being developed on the hoof by the Department of Social Security. But sooner or later Parliament will have to address the issue of common law marriage. Christians should be in the forefront of setting the criteria for any change in the law of marriage.

---

1 Rev. E.A. Pratt, St. Simon's Church, Festing Road, Southsea, Hants PO4 0NQ. (Available from the author @ £2.50 inc. postage)

The Issue of Cohabitation

There are basically three positions that Christians can take on the subject of cohabitation. A *rigorist* view is that cohabitation should be condemned along with all acts of pre-marital intercourse. On this view cohabitation is sin and always partakes of the nature of fornication where it is accompanied by sexual intercourse. The more typically Anglican viewpoint is *latitudinarian* and turns a blind eye to living together before marriage. It takes the view: Ask no questions and be told no lies. Better marriage than no marriage. I want to argue along with Forster and Jenkins for a *third way,* which tries to be compassionate but honest, biblical but affirming. This third way recognizes that there are many different types of cohabitation and that the Christian response should be basically a pastoral one. This open and sympathetic approach does not frighten people away as a more rigorist policy can tend to do, but offers the opportunity through marriage preparation to bring the gospel message to cohabiting couples.

The Facts of Cohabitation

A look at marriages contracted at my church over the past year is illuminating about the prevalence of cohabitation in this part of the South-East England. Ten couples were married in church, of whom four gave the same address for bride and bridegroom on their banns application forms. I have reasons for believing that, of the remaining six couples, three were living together despite different addresses. This means that some 70% of couples seeking marriage at this town church were probably cohabitating.

There are of course many different types of cohabiting relationships. In speaking of cohabitation we are talking about heterosexual couples living together outside of marriage, usually with a shared house or flat, a common purse and varying degrees of sexual intimacy. For some it is a *casual sexual relationship,* perhaps one of a succession of promiscuous unions. For others it partakes of the nature of a *'trial marriage'* in which the couple experiment to see whether the relationship will prove satisfactory before entering into marriage. For others it is a *provisional relationship* intended to lead towards marriage when finance and other circumstances allow. For some it is an *alternative or substitute for legal marriage.*

We need to distinguish from cohabitation what the Dutch call LAT, Living-Apart-Together. Many young people, particularly students, have shared accommodation without any sexual relationship. This should caution us against drawing conclusions too hastily from a common address. The Board of Social Responsibility has defined a *cohabiting union* as one where a man and a woman in a sexual relationship have lived together at the same address for six months or more. I believe that six months is too short and this period should be extended to at least twelve months.[1] Cohabiting unions like marriages exhibit the whole spectrum of relationships from the casual and unstable to the committed and permanent. In England, as in France and

---

[1] *Cohabitation: A Report from the Board of Social Responsibility.* (GS Misc. 391). The Rowntree Survey found that one third of cohabiting couples had been living together for less than one year. On the other hand 16% of cohabiting couples had lived together for more than five years. It also found that cohabiting couples with children tended to be socially disadvantaged in terms of employment, income support and housing. Social Policy Research Findings, May 1993.

Germany, it seems that for many cohabitation tends to be a temporary phase leading to marriage.

It was the Scandinavian countries, Sweden, Denmark and Iceland, which led the way into the cohabitation lifestyle in the 1960s. At that time the number of couples cohabiting in England was small and they were often divorcees. Statistics from the Office of Population Censuses and Surveys show that in 1972, 16% of women had lived with their husbands prior to marriage. By 1987 this proportion had risen dramatically to about 50%.[1] It seems that the past tendency for people in cohabiting unions to marry when the woman became pregnant is less apparent today. Increasing numbers of young women are having children whilst cohabiting. In 1990, births outside of marriage totalled 200,000, which were some 28.3% of total live births. 73% of extra-marital births were registered by both parents, and in nearly three out of four cases the parents gave the same address. But despite cohabitation the number of single-parent families in Britain has doubled during the past 20 years to a total of 1.15 million[2].

A survey in Britain showed that 43% of men and women favoured living together before marriage, as compared with 37% who advised going direct into marriage.[3] However the lowest rates of cohabitation are found amongst regular churchgoers.[4] Scotland and Wales have rates of cohabitation half that of England. In contrast with England, the incidence of cohabitation in Ireland, the Mediterranean countries and Eastern Europe is negligible, although it seems to be on the increase.

Despite the prevalence of cohabitation, marriage is still held in high regard in this country, although there does seem to be evidence that the number choosing to remain single is rising.[5] In a European Values Study in 1990, 81% of the British respondents disagreed with the notion that marriage was outdated. This contrasted with only 66% affirming the relevance of marriage in France.[6] But modern marriages carry much higher expectations than those of previous generations. In the 1950s the roles of breadwinner and homemaker were regarded as the most important for husband and wife respectively. Thirty-five years later the most important qualities stressed in marriage were mutual respect and appreciation, faithfulness, understanding and tolerance and a happy sexual relationship. Income and housing come well down the scale.[7] J.R. Gillis writes:

'People expect more of the conjugal relationship. It is made to bear the full weight of needs for intimacy, companionship, and love, needs which were previously met in other ways. Couples expect more of one another.'[8]

The high cost of modern weddings is a deterrent against getting married. The high

---

1 *Social Trends 22* (HMSO 1992), cited in GS Misc 391.
2 Duncan Dormor: article in *The Independent*, 10.2.92.
3 J. Scott 1990, cited in D.J. Dormor *The Relationship Revolution: Cohabitation, Marriage and Divorce in Contemporary Europe*, (One Plus One, 1992), p. 15.
4 Clayton & Voss 1977, cited in Dormor *op. cit.* p. 15.
5 The number of marriages per 1,000 between eligible bachelors and spinsters declined by about 40% in the eleven years from 1973 to 1984. The numbers of marriages in England and Wales remained remarkably stable during the 1980s. This is accounted for by the growing numbers of second and third marriages. Such marriages show no greater stability than first marriages.
6 Dormor *op. cit.* p. 19.
7 Dormor *op. cit.* p. 21.
8 *For Better, For Worse: British Marriages, 1600 to the Present,* (Oxford University Press, Oxford, 1985), p. 318.

level of divorce is a further reason often cited by young people who favour cohabiting unions in preference to marriage. Too often they have witnessed the breakdown of their parents or relatives' marriages. At one time there were financial advantages in not getting married. But these were largely removed in 1988 when the right of cohabiting couples to claim double tax relief on mortgage interest payments was removed. However a divorced woman still stands to lose pension rights from a previous marriage when she remarries.

Against this it should be noted that in the absence of a legal contract cohabitants can lose money and property when they separate. 'Extracting oneself from a cohabiting relationship can be even more complicated than divorce,' says Coventry solicitor, Jill Bowler. 'The court has limited powers to adjust the parties' ownership of property. It can only decide on the evidence, who actually owns what by purchase, gift or contributions.' [1] The legal disadvantages of cohabitation are spelt out more fully later in this booklet.

It should not surprise us that cohabiting relationships are often less stable than marriages. In Sweden a cohabiting union is six times as likely to break up as a marriage. Similar evidence has emerged from the Netherlands. Nor does subsequent marriage show much stability. This is confirmed by a recent study by the Office of Population, Censuses and Surveys. It shows that couples who live together before getting married are up to 60% more likely to get divorced than those who do not. The figures collected in *Population Trends* reveal a steady upward trend. Whereas in 1970-75 those who had lived together were 30% more likely to divorce after five years than those who had not cohabited, that figure had risen to 50% for those married between 1980 and 1984. After eight years of marriage the difference in the 1980s rose to 60%. Duncan Dormor of the 'One Plus One' research project (headed by Dr. Jack Dominian at the Central Middlesex Hospital) writes:

'Whilst the report says the results do not establish a causal link between pre-marital cohabitation and divorce, it identifies some common factors, such as that couples who have a religious ceremony stay longer than those who have a civil marriage. The authors believe the two main possible reasons for the trend are that couples who live together before marriage are less likely to think of it as a life-long commitment, and that such couples are more likely to be unconventional in their beliefs, and thus more likely to consider divorce.' [2]

Duncan Dormor's recent study on the extent and effects of cohabitation makes for sober reading. His conclusions may be summarized as follows:

(1) In Western Europe living together before marriage will soon become a majority practice. Currently half of those marrying for the first time in England and Wales cohabit first. By the year 2000, this could increase to four out of five couples.

(2) It is likely that cohabitation will become a common stage of late courtship, although people may well go through a series of cohabitations before entering one which leads to marriage.

(3) Increasingly cohabitation rather than marriage will become the context for child-bearing.

(4) Marriage is likely to decline except for those with religious convictions or those who wish to affirm their commitment to each other.

---

1 *Reader's Digest*, December 1992, p. 114.
2 Article in *The Independent*, 19.6.92.

(5) The decline in marriages may well be reflected in a corresponding fall in the divorce rate.

(6) It is likely that people will have a succession of different relationships whether outside or within marriage, so that some form of serial monogamy will become commonplace in many European countries.

(7) The decline in stable relationships will mean that increasing numbers of children will be brought up in single parent households headed by a woman. Many children will be brought up without regular contact with their fathers. It will be an increasingly matrilineal society.[1]

1
The Biblical Evidence

If cohabitation is a fact of life amongst more than half of the population which seeks to enter into marriage, how should Christians regard the practice? Is it always to be treated as a sinful relationship? Does it sometimes partake of the nature of a marriage, and if so where should we draw the boundaries? What guidelines can we draw from Scripture?

How then does a marriage come into being? The Bible tells us that it was not good for man to be alone. But no suitable mate could be found for Adam, so God created Eve. Adam said 'This at last is bone of my bone and flesh of my flesh', because Eve was made out of one of the man's ribs as a special creation. It goes on to relate the foundation of the institution of marriage in these words:

'Therefore a man leaves his father and mother and cleaves to his wife, and they become one flesh.' (Genesis 2.24).

This is one of the creation ordinances of Scripture, which by its position in the story of the first beginnings of human society is intended to be of universal application. It speaks of a monogamous union between a man and his wife. This union is marked by a departure from the authority of the parental home to the setting up of a new family unit (the leaving). The Hebrew word, *dabaq* for 'cleave' literally means 'to adhere to'. This sense of gluing together is underlined by the same word being used in 2 Samuel 23.10 (where the hand of Eleazar 'cleaved' to the sword after a day of battle) and in Job 19.20 (where the bones of Job 'cleave' to his skin and his flesh). The leaving and the cleaving is consummated by the one flesh bonding, which is at the same time a sexual, psychological and spiritual union.

When Jesus comments on this seminal passage in Matthew 19.3-12, he makes it clear that marriage is a monogamous and exclusive relationship, which is intended by God to be permanent and lifelong. However Jesus does recognize divorce as a divine concession to human weakness (for 'your hardness of heart'). He declares that *porneia* (i.e. adultery or other grave sexual offence) is the ground for marriage dissolution. What is noteworthy about the foundational text in Genesis 2.24 is that it makes no mention whatever of any *ceremony* of marriage. Marriage is complete when there is

---

1 Dormor *op. cit.* p. 31.

a leaving, a cleaving and a coming together as 'one flesh'. This view is confirmed by passages such as Genesis 24.67, where we are told that Isaac brought Rebecca 'into his tent, and took (her) and she became his wife, and he loved her'.

Throughout Scripture we can search in vain for any one particular ceremony constituting a marriage. There are two references in the Old Testament to a man covering a woman with his skirt (Ruth 3.9; Ezekiel 16.8). This was generally the act of a kinsman offering the woman his protection, taking her into his house and effectively making her a wife. This could be accompanied by some kind of marriage agreement. In the Mishnah the marriage contract drawn up by the father of the bride is called the *ketuba* (Tobit 7.14). Tobit is worth reading for the delightful description of the consummation of the marriage between Tobias and Sarah (Tobit 7 and 8). Biblical marriages were often accompanied by feasting and other social activities. Jesus attended a marriage feast at Cana (John 2); a king gives a marriage feast for his son (Matthew 22); and the wise and foolish virgins are part of the wedding party celebrating the procession of the bridegroom to the home of the bride (Matthew 25). We can also glean from Scripture that the bride and bridegroom would sometimes wear embroidered garments, especially in a royal marriage (Ps. 45.13-14; Is. 61.10), and that the guests were expected to dress in festal robes (Matt. 22.11-12).

The Apostle Paul affirms the sanctity of the marriage relationship in Ephesians 5 and tells the Church to 'walk in love as Christ loves us'. He then tells them that fornication and impurity must not even be named among them. It is in this context that he goes on to make the daring analogy between the love of Christ for the Church and the love of a husband for his wife. 'Husbands, love your wives, as Christ loved the church and gave himself up for her' (Eph. 5.25). Paul then like Jesus cites Genesis 2.24, and adds, 'This mystery is a profound one, and I am saying that it refers to Christ and the church' (Eph. 5.32). Paul is arguing that the bonding and 'one-fleshment' in the marriage relationship is a human picture of the divine bonding and enfleshment in the union between Christ and his bride, the Church.

The essential point about the biblical marriage practices is that the actual marriage was completed by the leaving, cleaving and bonding of the creation ordinance. As Greg Forster writes concerning Genesis 2.24:

> 'The definition of marriage implied by this aetiological narrative is that leaving the parental family and establishing a recognizable unit of one's own constitutes marriage, whether this is accompanied by an elaborate marriage or not.'[1]

The celebrations, the feasting, the processing and the like did not constitute a marriage, any more than the wedding reception and the honeymoon do today. We have to distinguish the essential biblical requirements of marriage from the incidental customs, norms and practices of any particular society or culture. The universality of the creation ordinance is that it is not tied to any particular time or place. The absence of any biblical presciption of what constitutes a marriage other than that of the creation ordinance allows for this universal approach. This means that where the creation ordinance is fulfilled there is a valid marriage in the view of Scripture. Even though the marriage may need to be regulated to comply with the particular legal norms of any one society, its validity is not compromised in the biblical perspective. A man and woman who fulfil the requirements of the creation ordinance are man and wife in the eyes of God.

---

1 *Marriage Before Marriage.* (Grove Ethical Studies No. 69), p. 14.

Gary Jenkins has argued that all sexual relationships are responses to the biblical norms of marriage.[1] He looks at cohabitation in terms of the biblical norms. He concludes that 'a cohabitating (or married) relationship falls short of God's intention to the extent that it is not based on love as God defines it; to the extent that it is not a permanent committed relationship; to the extent that its sexual expression does not express what God intends it to express; to the extent that the relationship lacks a full and proper community dimension; to the extent that the place of children in the relationship is not fully recognized; and to the extent to which the couple do not have the freedom that comes to those who live and love in the way that God intended.'[2] Jenkins's analysis is valuable in stressing the place of love and commitment and other ingredients of a lasting relationship between a man and woman. But it is worth pointing out that these qualities which are in large measure subjective may be present or absent in both legal marriages and in cohabiting unions. They are ideals and cannot in themselves form the basis of marriage law and practice.

If we can accept that marriage in the biblical sense is constituted by a leaving, cleaving and bonding, then we should want to see national law brought into line with the biblical norm. It may be more difficult to establish the boundaries of marriage in the absence of a special ceremony, but it is by no means beyond the capacity of legislation as I shall suggest later. Having said this I am well aware how easy it is to misrepresent the position for which I am arguing. I am not seeking to encourage cohabitation outside of a proper legal framework. Those who find themselves in a cohabiting relationship should still be urged to regulate that relationship within the current marriage laws. Christian young couples should still be warned against the danger of falling into a cohabiting relationship.

2
The Pastoral Approach

What are the practical and pastoral consequences of the three approaches that we have discussed? At the outset though it needs to be recognized that an incumbent in the Church of England *is obliged* to marry all those who fulfil the resident requirements in his parish. The legal position is that persons who are legally qualified to intermarry (ie. they are not married to anybody else, they are at least 16 years of age, and if under 18 years have parental consent, and are not within the prohibited degrees of consanguinity or affinity) are entitled to be married according to the rites of the Church of England in the parish church where one of them has residence, or where one is on the church electoral roll of the parish.

The only exception to this general right of marriage in the parish church is that a clergyman is not obliged to marry a divorced person whose former spouse is still living.[3] A divorced person may be refused marriage in the parish church but not a

---

1 *Cohabitation: A Biblical Perspective,* (Grove Ethical Studies No. 84), p. 8.
2 Jenkins *op. cit.* p. 19.
3 Halsbury *Ecclesiastical Law,* 1975, para. 1003.

person who has cohabited with a third person. I have had the absurd situation of being approached about marriage by a couple where the man was a divorcee and the woman a mother of a young daughter. Even though the man's marriage had collapsed within months, he was not entitled to marriage in the parish church. But his intended wife, who had cohabited with another man for several years and borne his child, could not legally be refused marriage to another qualified person.

The right of marriage in the parish church applies even to persons who are not members of the Church of England.[1] The Legal Adviser to General Synod in 1986 gave his opinion that even where both parties are unbaptized a claim to be married cannot be lawfully refused in the case of marriage by banns.[2] Furthermore under the Matrimonial Causes Act 1965, a minister who without just cause refuses to marry persons entitled to be married in his church commits an ecclesiastical offence for which he may be punished in the ecclesiastical courts.[3]

I personally consider that this obligation upon an incumbent to marry all and sundry within his parish without their having any professed Christian faith, or even if they practise some other religion,[4] is very unsatisfactory and in need of reform. It is a hangover from the days when clerks in holy orders were an extension of the state's bureaucracy. The whole business of banns and the registration of marriages by the clergy is an anomaly. My favoured preference would be to follow the practice of numerous European states and require all marriages to be registered by the civil authority with the option of a Christian marriage service in church to follow afterwards.[5]

How in practice should a Christian minister treat couples who are cohabiting? As a minister I have found myself having frequent pastoral contact with young couples living together. I soon learnt not to assume that living together meant that a couple were married. Equally I learnt not to assume that young people living under the same roof were necessarily having a sexual relationship. I have found that one has to be very cautious and pragmatic. How do I regard for example a couple who approach me about the baptism of a child when I discover that they not legally married? I could take a hardline view and refuse baptism on the grounds of cohabitation. But would I be justified in so doing on that ground alone, especially when I sometimes observe a level of love and commitment amongst cohabitants to each other which is often lacking in many legal marriages?

Of course there is a whole spectrum of relationships from the casual, through the provisional, to the committed. I have a friend of my age who has lived with a woman for almost as long as I have been married. The couple have had two children but despite a relationship of some thirty years or so, they have never been legally

---

1 R. v. James (1850) 3 Car & Kir 167 at 172, 175, CCR, per Alderson B.

2 Cited in *An Honourable Estate*, GS 801, 1988, pp. 81-84.

3 Matrimonial Causes Act 1965, s.8 (2).

4 The House of Bishops have issued guidelines for mixed faith marriages in Church. These recognize the general right of any parishioner of whatever faith to be married in the parish church, but stress that the minister should look for an understanding of the Christian teaching about marriage and not vary from the prescribed marriage service, e.g. by omitting Trinitarian references.

5 This option was considered by the Working Party which produced *An Honourable Estate*. It was rejected not so much on theological grounds, but on the pragmatic one that it would deprive the church of a mission opportunity. I personally doubt this conclusion and feel that the Church's opportunity to teach the Christian understanding of marriage would be increased if ministers were granted a limited discretion over marriage in church.

married. I find it impossible to regard a couple in such a relationship as other than man and wife. But equally when I find other couples who have lived together for a lesser period but are obviously living in a committed and loving relationship, which may or may not have produced children, I have to regard them as man and wife in a 'common law marriage'.

Greg Forster argues that the recognition of cohabiting unions does not legitimize fornication nor encourage immorality. He suggests that if a cohabiting relationship exhibits the features of married life, it is functionally a marriage. Such a relationship:

'may be in anticipation of a formal and legal marriage ceremony, or as an alternative to it. If such cohabitation functions as one of the marriage customs of our culture, and if non-ecclesiastical celebrations (such as that in a Register Office in England or by Declarator in Scotland) are accepted by Christians as valid, then sexual activity within it is not fornication.'[1]

But Forster is honest enough to admit that there is inevitably 'a morally ambiguous beginning' to most if not all cohabiting relationship.

Over the years many committed couples have come to me saying that they wish to formalize their relationship by 'getting married'. After due enquiry I have tried to say something like this to such couples: 'I regard your relationship as that of man and wife. Under the creation ordinance of Genesis 2, you are married in the eyes of God. In another age, you might have been regarded as married under English common law. You are not however recognized as married according to current English law. It is right that you should seek to regularize your relationship by undergoing a marriage ceremony. This will regulate your relationship in law, giving you both the protection and security of a legal marriage. It will remove any ambiguity about the status of your children. It will provide an opportunity for your relationship to be publicly recognized and celebrated by your family and friends. Finally in coming to church you are asking for God's blessing and grace to rest upon your marriage and family.' This then provides a marvellous opportunity to explain to the couple the Christian understanding of marriage. From then the minister can go on to speak of the gospel message and the place of Christ in a true Christian marriage.

Perhaps we may compare this approach with the one that Edward Pratt proposes. Pratt states that cohabiting couples need to be prepared for marriage in a different manner from other couples. Pratt is insistent that cohabiting couples must be faced with the need to repent. For him the best way of demonstrating this repentance is to require the couple to live apart until the wedding day. This seems to me to be a confusion. Repentance and faith are indeed the way that every sinner must take if he wants to come to Christ. But why single out cohabitants for special treatment? Other couples may come to marriage with a whole history of promiscuous relationships behind them that we never learn about. Even if we concede for the purposes of the argument that the cohabiting relationship began with an act of fornication, we have to recognize that this is the case in most marriages today. For it is said that less than 10% of brides are virgins, and presumably the same goes for bridegrooms! And I would want to say that where a couple take a considered act to live together in a committed relationship, they are fulfilling the criteria of marriage according to the creation ordinance and we have no right to lay upon them the obligation to live apart.

---

1 Forster *op. cit.* p. 15.

An alternative that Pratt suggests, particularly where the cohabitants have a child, is to include a reference to the couple's repentance in the wedding sermon or in a prayer. Pratt gives examples in an appendix, as well as some suggestions about what to say when a couple are not repentant about cohabitation.[1] Pratt admits that the majority of such couples are unrepentant, and that he tells them that they would be better to marry in a register office. He also wants to exercise church discipline against cohabitants by denying them baptism (and the baptism of their children) and confirmation and communion without repentance.

Edward Pratt invited contributions from parents who were facing the problem of children living in cohabiting relationships. This particularly presents parents with the problem as to whether to allow the couple to stay the night with them, and whether to offer them separate or joint bedrooms. Christian parents find different responses to this kind of issue. One married couple wrote about the contrast between one of their three children who got married and the other two who were still cohabiting. They wrote: 'This marriage...and our closer relationship with our new daughter-in-law have highlighted the less fulfilled relationships of our other children, and the feeling that their common-law spouses do not "belong" to our family.' Another mother wrote that she welcomed her daughter and cohabiting boy-friend warmly to her home, but would only visit them in their home as individuals and would not stay for a meal. This same mother would only give personal gifts and not gifts which were for the couple to use in their home. One wonders how long this kind of distinction can be maintained.

I can quite understand the anguish suffered by Christian parents in this whole area. I hope that nothing that I have said can be construed as encouraging pre-marital intercourse. Parents must still teach their children the importance of chastity before marriage and fidelity within marriage. It should be the prayer of Christian parents that their children would be virgins when they enter into marriage. But we all know the enormous media and peer pressures upon young people today. Whatever our teaching and good intentions the evidence suggests that many children from Christian homes are going to fail to live up to Christian standards of sexual behaviour. I believe that whilst we must not compromise our beliefs, we have to show love, compassion and acceptance to our children however often they fall. We must surely avoid conduct which appears to be judgmental and rejecting. I hope that whatever boundaries we set, we will not separate ourselves from our children. Jesus ate and drank with sinners. Taylorite Closed Brethren will not eat with unbelievers or even those outside their sect. We must follow the Jesus way and not the path of religious prejudice however well intentioned.[2]

So far as church life is concerned, Sunday School and church youth groups must go on teaching youngsters the continuing importance of avoiding sexual intercourse before marriage. Virginity should be the goal of all Christian young people entering into marriage. They also need to be assured that they are not missing out in steering clear of sexual relationships before marriage and given every pastoral support to stand against the prevailing sexual youth culture. We will discover from time to time Christian couples living together in a cohabiting union. We should not fall into the

---

1 *Living in Sin?* Appendix B, C & D.
2 Paul tells the Corinthian Christian to refrain from table fellowship with a brother or sister who is living in sin. He mentions the sexually immoral, but also includes those who are greedy, idolaters, revilers, robbers and drunkards! (I Cor. 5.11).

trap of judging such couples without a full knowledge of all the facts. Ill-judged church discipline may drive such couples away from Christian fellowship and support. It may well be that many such couples are living in the kind of settled and committed relationship which falls within the biblical norms of marriage according to the creation ordinance. We can however impress upon such couples the need publicly to regularize their relationship in a marriage ceremony. Such a ceremony is needed to satisfy the law of the land, to remove any uncertainty about the status of the relationship in the eyes of the church, and to give families and friends a legitimate and proper occasion to celebrate a new family unit. So there are legal, social, ecclesial and familial reasons for the public recognition of a cohabiting union as a marriage relationship.

3

The General Synod Debate

General Synod debated the issue of cohabitation at York in July 1992. It came before the Synod on a private member's motion from Canon Michael Walker (St. Edmundsbury and Ipswich). His motion read:

'This Synod, recognizing that it is now an accepted custom in England for couples to live together before marriage, whilst others express the intention never to be formally married, request (sic) the House of Bishops to give moral guidance to the nation concerning the nature of Christian marriage today, and pastoral guidance to the clergy as they seek to minister to parishioners in this situation.'

Canon Walker pointed to the high incidence of cohabitation as the reason for initiating this debate. He said that even in a respectable and traditional area like Bury St. Edmunds, half of those coming for a church wedding were already living together. Clergy from other parts of the country had reported figures as high as 90%.

Canon Walker wanted the Bishops to give a clear statement as to where the Church stands. 'Unless people have a recognized standard by which to measure their lives, the breakdown in morals will be total. Already it may be too late and Christian moral standards may be laughed out of court.' He asked for answers to these questions: is cohabitation before marriage sinful? If it is sinful what should our attitude be to those living this sort of life and how should we respond if and when they do decide to get married? If cohabitation is not sinful, were we mistaken in the past when we described that relationship as 'living in sin'?

For some the issue was quite simple. Mr. Gerald O'Brien (Chelmsford) said that the Bible only recognizes two states, being single and being married. As pre-marital and extra-marital sexual activity was proscribed, it followed that cohabitation was sinful. 'Sometimes the Church of England and this Synod should not be afraid to call sin sin.' But this rigorist approach did not find favour from Canon Tony Chesterman (Derby). For him what mattered was not whether a couple were married or cohabiting but the quality of the relationship. He did not approve of the motion which he thought sounded 'like an embarrassed Church talking not to the nation but to itself'. The Rev. Martin Flatman (Oxford) thought that we should be very careful when it came to sin. 'We all live in sin. We are all committing sins all over the place, all the time. This obsession with sex as the only sin is a lot of nonsense. We all have to face sin; we all have to come before God and say "I am messing up my life in one way or another" '.

Most speakers were anxious not to treat cohabitation in a legalistic but in a pastoral fashion. The Rev. Dr. David Ison (Coventry) told of a number of horror stories. One young couple asking for marriage admitted to the vicar that they were living together. The Vicar said 'How dare you be so hypocritical as to walk down the aisle in a white dress pretending to be a virgin? Go away. I don't want anything more to do with you.' He knew of at least one church where the children of cohabiting parents are refused baptism unless the parents get married first. It was said that the parents could not make the baptismal promise 'I repent of my sins' when they continued to live in sin. Another woman of his acquaintance had said that God would condemn her if she did not warn a cohabitant of her sin. 'When she had said what she had to say to the woman who was cohabiting, she walked off and left her sobbing.' It was no doubt with such examples in mind that the Bishop of Bath and Wells said 'Those clergy who are receiving people who have been cohabiting and who immediately reject them should change their practice here and now.'

One of the most moving speeches in the debate came from the Rev. Gavin Reid (Guildford), shortly afterwards to be consecrated Bishop of Maidstone. 'For me cohabitation is not someone else's problem, it is my problem. It is very close to home and affecting members of my family.' He went on to say that there is sin in cohabitation. 'There is in cohabitation a serious departure from what is best for people, and sin is a departure from what is best. I believe that it is fundamentally a sin against the community. It is a form of privatization in human affairs. It fails to recognize that we are social beings and that a stable society needs to order its relationships.' Nevertheless Gavin Reid wanted to stress that the essence of marriage was the leaving and cleaving of the creation ordinance in Genesis 2.24. He added:

'We must work out an attractive apologia for marriage in the sight of the community. We will not help ourselves by adopting the view that marriages are made in churches or registry (sic) offices: that is not where marriages are made. Christians need to insist on the profundity and the life-changing aspect of sexual intercourse. If two people cohabit and try to avoid placing themselves within the expectations of the community, I believe that it is our duty as Christians to put these expectations on those people and hold them to the bond that they have created, whether they like it or not.'

Because Gavin Reid wanted to make cohabiting unions into permanent and binding unions, he was against parents discriminating against such couples, as for example by not giving presents for the home but only for individuals as suggested by one correspondent in the CEN. He was likewise opposed to a penitential addition to the marriage service. 'That would be pastorally disastrous; it would deter, when we are wanting to make people do the opposite. Why let all the others off the hook, and blame the people who have openly slept together?'

Another effective and informed speech came from Mrs. Diana Johnson (Peterborough). She began by hazarding a guess that in 20 years' time many of their successors in the Synod, including the clergy, would have had the experience of living with their partner before marriage. She went on to point out how marriage without a ceremony was valid until 1563 under Catholic canon law and until 1753 under English civil law. She claimed that in the nineteenth century it was rare for a working class couple to go through a marriage ceremony at all. In Shaw's *Pygmalion*, Arthur Doolittle only persuades the woman he is living with to marry him when he comes into money. He explains to Colonel Pickering that she has changed her mind because of their new circumstances. 'Intimidated, guv'nor. Intimidated. Middle class morality claims its victim. Respectability 'as broke all the spirit out of 'er.'

She echoed Gavin Reid in not wanting to put any barriers in the way of those, 'who whatever their previous living arrangements, have come to the point where they want to make their commitment to God and to each other in church.' For her own sons she wanted them to find 'a marriage of openness, intimacy, sexual fulfilment and the pursuit of personal signficance', as Jack Dominian has defined the goals of modern marriage. 'Yes I trust them to behave with thought, care and integrity. If that means that they choose to live with someone, so be it. They will have my love and support. If they go on to get married, they will have my blessing and I shall rejoice greatly.' Mrs. Sue Page (Norwich) wanted to establish betrothal as a first stage of public commitment to cohabitation before marriage.

In the end the Synod decided to take a more cautious and less speedy course than that advocated by Canon Walker. It adopted a revised motion moved by the Bishop of Bath and Wells in the following terms:

> 'This Synod, noting the increased incidence in which couple are living together outside of marriage and concerned to sustain the institution of marriage and the family, welcome (sic) the study of the family being conducted by the Board of Social Responsibility and invite the House of Bishops to consider, when the deliberations of the Board's Working Party are available, what further guidance to issue to the Church and nation.'

4

A Brief Account of Marriage Law in England

Prior to the Council of Trent in 1563, Roman Canon law required no religious ceremony. The overriding consideration was that marriages should be entered into with the free consent of both parties. All that was necessary for a valid marriage was a declaration by the parties that they took each other as husband and wife. This could be done in the form of an espousal (*per verba de praesenti* e.g. 'I take you as my wife/husband)', in which case the marriage was binding immediately, or by way of a betrothal (*per verba de futuro* e.g. 'I shall take you as my wife/husband'), in which case the marriage was complete as soon as it was consummated. But this system provided no proper safeguards against bigamous or incestuous unions or the marriage of minors, and tended not to be used where property was involved. The Church encouraged marriage *in facie ecclesiae* after banns (or the issue of a papal or episcopal licence) and with the consent of the parents of those under 21 years. Such a church marriage would be conducted at the church door *per verba de praesenti* in the presence of the priest, after which the couple would generally go into the church for the celebration of a nuptial mass. Chaucer's Wife of Bath declares that she has been properly married six times at the church door.

The Reformation made no basic change in the marriage law. The Book of Common Prayer 1552 required that the ceremony should take place in the body of the church between the couple to be married in the company of their friends and neighbours. There in the presence of the priest they should give their consent, make their vows and exchange a ring. This was basically marriage *per verba de praesenti in facie ecclesiae* in which the celebrants of the marriage were the bridegroom and bride with the minister and congregation being the witnesses. Only when the minister had declared the couple man and wife, did the civil part of the marriage conclude and the strictly religious part of the marriage continue with the husband and wife kneeling at the Lord's table for the prayers.[1] These two parts of the ceremony are retained in the 1980 ASB Marriage Service.

But until 1753 marriages did not have to be church marriages. There were also *clandestine marriages* made *per verba de praesenti* before a clerk in holy orders.[2] A whole class of clergy, known as Fleet parsons, made a flourishing living out of this kind of marriage. Because there was no registration of such a marriage, unscrupulous bigamists and heiress hunters rendered such unions notorious. Finally there could be a union *per verba praesenti*, or *per verba de futuro* with subsequent consummation. Such common law marriages were valid for most purposes, although not effective for transferring a wife's property to her husband. Common law marriages were, like all other marriages, treated as indissoluble and therefore rendered void any subsequent marriage.

Lord Hardwicke's Act of 1753 was passed to stop the abuse of clandestine marriages. It required that the only legal marriage (except for Jews or Quakers) was one conducted by banns or licence according to the rites of the Church of England in the parish church in the presence of a clergyman and two other witnesses. It thus rendered unnecessary the power of the Ecclesiastical Courts to compel a clandestine or common law marriage to be celebrated *in facie ecclesiae*. Lord Hardwicke's Act, as amended by the Marriage Act, 1823, remained the law for nearly two hundred years. Its discrimination against Roman Catholics, Nonconformists and non-Christians was progressively removed. The Marriage Act 1836 allowed a purely civil marriage before a registrar of marriages and two witnesses. The superintendent registrar could issue certificates to marry in a registered building which could be a non-Anglican chapel or church. The Marriage Act 1898 allowed the ministers of all religious denominations similar powers to an Anglican minister to solemnize marriage without the presence of a marriage registrar. All the marriage laws were consolidated by the Marriage Act 1949.

Following Lord Hardwicke's Act, English couples could only escape the tight provisions of the law by eloping to Scotland. There over the blacksmith's anvil at Gretna Green, they would make a declaration that they took each other as husband and wife. Scottish law then and now allows marriages *per verba de praesenti*. In addition it seems that where a couple are known as husband and wife 'by habit and repute', and have lived together over a number of years, they may be treated as legally married. It

---

1 During the Commonwealth, marriages could be celebrated before a J.P.
2 They were called clandestine marriages because they were contrary to the canons of 1604, which forbade marriage other than in church.

appears that there are a dozen or so cases a year in which the Scottish Court of Session is asked to confirm that such a common law marriage exists or existed.[1]

The Legal Differences Between Cohabitation and Marriage

The difference in legal status between cohabitants and married partners is not generally appreciated. Although there has been a progressive whittling away at the distinctions, particularly through the operation of the Social Security system, there remain substantial differences. In a number of important areas the position of a cohabitant is vulnerable. This is particularly the case in matters of property and finance. Not only does a cohabitant stand in a potentially adverse position in regard to the common home and household goods, but s/he can also lose out significantly on inheritance. Some couples seek to protect their respective rights and obligations through a cohabitation agreement. These arrangements may set out the rights to the home and possessions and the position of children in the event of a break-up in the relationship. However it is doubtful if such contracts are enforceable in law since they lack 'valuable consideration', that is to say that they are not for money or money's worth. It is possible to protect a partner's interest by entering both partners' names on a joint tenancy agreement or conveyance. Similarly money can be held at the bank in joint names.

In a marriage children are the joint parental responsibility of both parents. But an unmarried mother has the sole parental responsibility for her children unless she makes a voluntary parental responsibility agreement with the father, or he applies to the court for a parental responsibility order. Unlike a husband the male partner is not presumed to be the father. In the event of a breakdown in the cohabitation, the mother can apply to the court for a maintenance order against her male partner for the support of the child (an affiliation order), but she must prove that he is the father.[2] On the other hand a male partner has no automatic right of access to the child unless he applies to the court for an order. The same situation exists where the mother dies. A child can inherit from both married parents, but a child of unmarried parents would have to prove parentage if s/he is to inherit under an intestacy, that is where there is no will. Cohabiting couples are not allowed to adopt a child jointly, although a single partner may adopt in certain circumstances.

A wife may sue her husband for failure to be maintained by her husband. If they are separated she may apply for a maintenance order from a magistrates' court. Where there is no marriage, a woman has no right to sue her male partner for maintenance. But as we have seen, she may get what used to be called a paternity order against him for the maintenance of any children of the partnership. A widow's pension or widowed mother's allowance is paid to a married woman on the death of her husband but not to a cohabiting woman. Similarly most occupational pension schemes exclude cohabitants. Since Sixth April 1990 husbands and wives are taxed separately so there is no difference in the tax regime as between them and cohabitants. The old discrimination against married couples in only being able to claim a single tax relief for the purchase of the matrimonial home was abolished in 1988. Previously there was an

---

1 J. Rees: Article 'For Better - or Worse' in *Church Times*, 20 August 1982, cited by Greg Foster: *Marriage Before Marriage?* p. 11.
2 The newly created Child Support Agency is given wide powers to pursue fathers for the maintenance of their children. But single mothers are expected to name the father of their child.

incentive for couples not to marry so that they could each claim tax relief, pushing their joint relief up to £60,000, double the amount for husbands and wives. There is a presumption in marriage that possessions are owned jointly. But no such presumption operates in a cohabiting relationship where ownership of household goods rests with the one who bought them or was given them.

In a marriage both partners have a right to occupy the matrimonial home unless one is excluded by court order, such as a husband for violence against his wife. If there is a divorce, the court will generally divide the proceeds of the matrimonial home equally between the couple in the absence of special circumstances. But a cohabitant has no legal right to the occupation or the ownership of the common home unless his or her name is on the tenancy or conveyance. In the absence of a joint tenancy or freehold ownership, the cohabitant is a mere licensee and may be required to leave the property without notice. This is subject to the qualification that a cohabitant may be able to prove a joint tenancy where both partners moved in together. The court also retains power to make an order for the transfer of the tenancy where there are children involved. Local authorities increasingly offer joint tenancies to cohabiting couples. Certain councils may also allow a cohabiting partner not named in the tenancy to remain in council property after the death or departure of the tenant.

If either partner to a cohabiting union dies without a will, the survivor has no general claim on the deceased's estate. In contrast to a widow who takes the major share on an intestacy (and the whole share if there are no children, parents, brothers, sisters, nephews or nieces), the cohabiting partner may get nothing. A cohabitant can claim where there is no will, but must show that s/he was dependent on, and maintained by, the other partner. Such a claim allows provision only for reasonable maintenance and not a share in the family assets. Where there is a will, the estate will be divided up according to its terms unless a claim is made under the Inheritance (Provision for Family and Dependants) Act 1975. Now a wife is entitled to claim not only provision for reasonable maintenance but also a 'fair share in the family assets.' But a cohabiting partner cannot claim under the Act.[1]

Where the Social Security system has intervened is in the award of benefits. If officers are satisfied that a couple are cohabiting, they will be treated as a couple in any claim for income support, family credit and housing benefit and their income assessed jointly. This is the so-called cohabitation rule, which is designed to place cohabitants in a no more favourable position than married couples. This rule has sometimes led to allegations of snooping by DSS officers. It can also sometimes affect unfairly couples who are residing together but not in any sense as husband and wives. Such couples (Living-Apart-Together) may have to persuade the DSS that they are not cohabitants. This can be important since the amount of benefit for a couple is usually less than for two single people.

---

1 e.g. in *CA* v. *CC* (1978) SJ 35: In 1972 a man started living with his mistress and adopted her daughter. In 1974 the couple had a son. In 1976 the man died not having revoked his 1971 will in which he had left all to an older son. His mistress applied to the court for a fair share of the estate. The Court of Appeal held that she was entitled to £5,000 for maintenance. The remainder of the estate valued at between £25,000 and £35,000 would be split between his two sons. The daughter received nothing.

5

Should Common Law Marriage Status be Granted to Cohabitants in Settled and Committed Relationships?

I want to argue the case for granting the status of common law marriage to cohabiting unions as a way of society seeking to shore up the institution of marriage and the family. I would propose that where a man and woman in a sexual relationship have lived together at the same address, or successive addresses, for twelve months or more, a common law marriage could come into being and be recognized as a legal marriage in one of the following ways:

(1) JOINT APPLICATION: By joint application of the cohabiting couple to the registrar of marriages for their union to be registered as a marriage. A sworn affadavit should be sufficient evidence for a common law marriage to be registered.

(2) EX PARTE APPLICATION: By application of one party to a court for a common law marriage to be recognized. This could be for a whole variety of reasons, such as to secure an equal share in the assets of the cohabiting union, or to obtain the custody of, or access to, a child of the union. In such a case the court could infer that a common law marriage existed from evidence such as a joint conveyance, mortgage or tenancy, or a joint bank account, or a joint registration of a child's birth.

As a matter of evidence a court would be able to draw a strong presumption of a common law marriage in two particular cases:

(i) COHABITATION CONTRACT: Where the parties to a cohabiting union have drawn up a contract to regulate their union, and where the contract implicitly recognizes that a cohabiting union exists, a legal presumption would arise of a common law marriage. Such a presumption throws the onus of proof on the party seeking to deny that a marriage existed.

(ii) A CHILD OF THE UNION: Where a cohabiting couple have a child, a legal presumption would arise of a common law marriage.

In addition to these publicly registered and recognized common law marriages, it is probable that a fairly high proportion of cohabiting unions would be unregistered and unrecognized. However provided that such unions fulfilled the criteria of stability and commitment within an exclusive sexual relationship, they ought to be recognized by the Church as *biblical marriages,* even if not *legal marriages* under the law of the country. This is important because such cohabiting unions are likely to present themselves to clergy where couples are seeking to use the services of the church for the occasional offices of baptisms, marriages and funerals.

The history of English marriage law shows that there is a long tradition of espousal, or marriage *per verba de praesenti.* Where such marriages did not take place in a church or under the auspices of a clergyman, they were still lawful and might fairly be described as common law marriages. Even after Lord Hardwicke's Act of

1753 many of the working class and urban poor were joined by common law marriage. *An Honourable Estate* stated that one effect of the 1753 Act was to 'distance the Church from more private traditions of entering the married state..."Common law" liaisons survived longest among the the lowest social classes and in the boom towns where the social framework was less fixed'.[1]

We have seen that the basic biblical requirement for marriage is that the criteria of Genesis 2.24 should be met. Marriage according to the creation ordinance requires a leaving, a cleaving and a bonding. We have seen too that the clear tendency in our society is towards cohabitation. We may not approve of this. We may not think it the ideal route to marriage. But we cannot pretend that today it is not the rule rather than the exception. Christian pastoral theology must take seriously the fact that we live in a flawed and fallen world, but a world which is redeemable through the grace and mercy of God. Rather than seeking to stand like Canute against the irresistible social tide, the questions that require to be seriously addressed are these:

– Is the overriding need to support family life, and to seek the welfare of cohabitants and their children, not best advanced by the lawful recognition of common law marriages?

– Where a couple are living in a settled and committed relationship does it make sense either for the State or for the Church to regard them other than as man and wife?

Forster argues that circumstances exist where the couple's commitment to each other, and the functions their relationship serves, correspond to those 'found in marriage. To call such relationships marriage is not an encouragement to promiscuity. Sexual exclusiveness is one of the touchstones by which they may be measured.'[2] Forster goes on to suggest that there are strong moral and practical reasons why such a couple should go on to matrimony, or, as I would express it, to the formal public registration or recognition of their marital status. This does not mean that Christian young people should in any way be encouraged to enter into cohabiting relationships. But it does mean that cohabitants will not feel themselves to be treated by the Church as lepers and outcasts.

What has been called the ambiguous nature of the beginnings of most, if not all, cohabiting relationships should warn us that cohabatation is not an option to be readily countenanced by Christians. Christian teaching should go on stressing the need to keep oneself pure for marriage. The honeymoon and not the courtship is the time for sexual experimentation. Nevertheless because we have to deal with our fallen humanity, Christians must avoid hasty judgments upon the actions of Christians and non-Christians in this area. Speculative sawdust in another's eyes so often blinds us to the plank in our own eye. Honesty requires us to admit that today there is frequently a morally ambiguous start to the relationship of many couples who come to church for marriage.

If a cohabiting couple under the present law (or under a reformed marriage law as advocated in this paper) come to a minister seeking, for example, the baptism of their child, how should he or she respond? An obvious pastoral difficulty is how to judge the degree of stability in cohabiting unions. Many may feel that twelve months is too short a period to make an assessment. However we need to recognize that many who get married have not known each other for much longer a period. And judg-

---

1 p. 22.
2 Forster *op. cit.* p. 23.

ments about the stability of marital relationships are not something totally foreign to clergy in the parochial ministry. They have to make private assessments of this kind all the time. Furthermore if a couple are asking for the child of their union to be baptized it shows a measure of commitment to each other. It is true that only time will tell whether a relationship is provisional or permanent, but then again the same must be said about many marriages. In the final analysis it is clear that any pastoral policy must deal with people as we find them. This means that we have to deal with realities and not just ideals. We may seek to influence committed Christians. But we can be sure that moral declamations from pulpits about cohabitation are not likely to affect those on the fringes of church life and those who make no profession of Christian faith.

It can be fairly objected to cohabiting unions that they lack any public or community dimension. They represent what Gavin Reid has called the privatization of marriage. Marriage is meant to be a social institution and not just a private contract between two individuals. Cohabitation also deprives families and friends of the opportunity to celebrate the union of husband and wife. It leaves third parties confused or uncertain about the relationship. At the same time a perfectly proper and legitimate occasion for relatives and friends to get together for a jolly good party is denied them. It is not for nothing that many of the parables of Jesus concern wedding feasts, and that the climax of redemption in the Book of Revelation is the marriage feast of the Lamb with his bride, the Church.

But these objections do not invalidate the status of cohabiting unions as *biblical marriages*. Rather they emphasize the social reasons for the proper registration or recognition of common law marriages. Such marriages need an occasion to be properly celebrated in a style appropriate to the means of the couple. Equally they argue the pastoral case for ministers to recommend cohabiting couples to get their relationship registered or recognized. It would be in the public recognition or registration of common law marriages that the cohabiting couple would affirm, expressly or implicitly, the permanent and committed nature of their relationship. For without some act which brings the union into the public domain there is no safeguard against bigamous or incestuous unions.

Furthermore, if it be admitted that the track record of cohabiting unions is that they are less stable than legal marriages, their public registration would be a factor tending towards the buttressing up such unions. It needs, I think to be stressed, that the legitimization of common law marriages, far from undermining the institution of marriage, would be a measure to strengthen marriage and family life. It cannot be argued against such legitimisation of common law marriages, that current evidence suggests that marriages after cohabitation are more prone to breakdown that other marriages. The key point is that marriages are more stable than non-marital unions, so everything that can be done to bring cohabiting unions within the marriage laws of the country should be done.

The legal recognition of common law marriages would protect the property and financial interests of the parties in a cohabiting union. In particular it would mean that a woman in a cohabiting union would be able to claim maintenance for herself. She could be protected against being evicted by the man from the family home. She would also be able to claim a share in the sale of the family home if it is owned solely by the man. She would have a proper claim to a share in the family assets in the event of intestacy or being omitted from her partner's will. Common law marriages would therefore be placed in a position of total legal parity with all other marriages, whether contracted in a church or a register office. Registration of such common law marriages would mean that they could only be dissolved in a similar way to other marriages. In other words the parties would have to prove irretrievable breakdown within the terms of the Matrimonial Causes Act, 1973. The registration or recognition of cohabiting unions as legal marriages would therefore be a reforming measure advancing the cause of social justice and equity, particularly for women.

It remains a comparatively cheap and simple matter to get married in a register office or church. But it may well be that there are couples, some of whom may have cohabited for many years, who may feel inhibited about a public ceremony of marriage. Such a couple might choose to regularize their relationship by visiting a local solicitor and swearing or affirming an affadavit before him which would recognize the common law marriage and could be retrospective in its effect. For example a couple could state that they had been living together as man and wife for the past ten years. This would legitimize children born during that period.

Other couples who do not wish to go through a ceremony of marriage often wish to regularize their legal relationship by a cohabitation contract. As I have already stated, such contracts may well be unenforceable in the courts. Legislation could make them enforceable, but with the qualification that such a contract would create a presumption of common law marriage. If public policy is to uphold the place of marriage and family life, then it is not unreasonable for Parliament to place the legal obligations of marriage upon all, not least upon those who want the security of marriage relationships without the responsibilities of such status. A similar argument applies to the presumption of a common law marriage where there is a child of the union. In such a case public policy, which leans towards the legitimization and protection of children, can reasonably override the objection of the couple that they were being married without their consent.

Finally cohabitants, having lived together as husband and wife, should be entitled to the same legal rights as a married couple. So if a cohabiting woman, for example, applies to the courts for equal division of the family home and other assets after separation or bereavement, it should be within the power of the courts to put her in the same position as a married woman. It is again not unreasonable for a court to declare that a common law marriage did exist. This would impose upon the couple the same legal rights and obligations as in an ordinary marriage. However since such a declaration might be said to offend against the principle that a person must give his or her assent to marriage, the other partner in a separation should be entitled to ask the court to declare such a marriage disssolved.

Betrothal has been urged by some Christians as a way of recognizing the growth of cohabitation. I suppose that the attraction is that betrothal was a stage in the marriage process in biblical times. Mary was betrothed to Joseph when she gave birth to her first born son, Jesus (Matt. 1.18-20). In the Bible the betrothal was almost as binding as marriage itself. The betrothed couple were treated as effectively husband and wife, except that sexual intercourse was excluded. They were under the same obligations of fidelity as married couples. Betrothal was really a legal intermediate status for the payment of the bride-price. There are not many parallels between biblical betrothal and modern-day cohabitation. Certainly young people living together would not expect to be denied sexual relations whilst being bound in a legal obligation identical to marriage. It is possible that betrothal could be used as a kind of euphemism for young people living together. This might appeal to some. But it does not commend itself to me. It would be a fiction and would solve none of the problems associated with cohabitation.

6
Conclusions

1   Currently half of those getting married in England and Wales have lived together before marriage.

2   The numbers cohabiting shows every indication of continuing to rise steadily.

3   Cohabiting unions tend to be less stable than marriages.

4   Couples who marry after cohabitation are more likely to go through divorce than those who go straight into marriage.

5   Marriage in Scripture is completed by a leaving, cleaving and bonding according to the creation ordinance in Genesis 2.24 (we call this *biblical marriage*).

6   Jesus, building on the creation ordinance, emphasizes the permanent, lifelong and exclusively monogamous nature of marriage.

7   Neither in the OT or the NT is there any biblical prescription for any particular *ceremony* of marriage.

8   From the biblical point of view a man and woman who fulfil the requirements of the creation ordinance are man and wife in the sight of God.

9   Marriage according to the requirements of national law constitutes a *legal marriage*.

10 A *biblical marriage* may not satisfy at any one time the requirements of national law, but such a marriage should not be regarded as living in sin.

11 Sexual intercourse within a *biblical marriage* is not fornication. It is the natural God-given expression of the bonding of man and wife.

12 Many cohabiting unions today do not satisfy the criteria of a *legal marriage*, but may nevertheless constitute a *biblical marriage*.

7
Proposals

A   There is a strong case to be argued by biblical Christians for the legal recognition of **cohabiting unions** as **common law marriages.**

B   **Common law marriages** should be capable of being recognized by English law where a couple are shown to have been living together in a sexual relationship at the same address, or successive addresses, for twelve months or more.

C   Where a couple have lived together for twelve months or more, a **common law marriage** could be legally recognized in one of the following ways:

(1) JOINT APPLICATION: By joint application of the cohabiting couple to the registrar of marriages for their union to be registered as a marriage. A sworn affadavit should be sufficient evidence for a common law marriage to be registered. Such registration would be capable of retrospective force from the date of the beginning of the cohabiting union.

(2) EX PARTE APPLICATION: By application of one party to a court for a common law marriage to be recognized. This could be for a whole variety of reasons, such as to secure an equal share in the assets of the cohabiting union, or to obtain the custody of, or access to, a child of the union. A court could infer that a common law marriage existed from evidence such as a joint conveyance, mortgage or tenancy, a joint bank account, or a joint registration of a child's birth.

As a matter of evidence a court would be able to draw a strong presumption of a common law marriage in two particular cases:

(i) COHABITATION CONTRACT: Where the parties to a cohabiting union have drawn up a legal contract to regulate their union, and where the contract implicitly recognizes that a cohabiting union exists, a presumption would arise of a common law marriage. (This would require legislation to make such contracts enforceable).

(ii) CHILD OF THE UNION: Where the couple have a child of their union, a presumption would arise of a common law marriage.

D   In addition to the common law marriages under C above, which would be registered or recognized as *legal marriages,* there would remain numbers of cohabiting unions which were unregistered or unrecognized. Provided that such unions met the criteria of stability and commitment within an exclusive sexual relationship, such unions ought to be recognized by the Church as *biblical marriages,* even if not as *legal marriages* under the law of the land.

E   The Church should continue to teach and preach the virtues of chastity before marriage. It should seek to uphold virginity as the ideal preparation for marriage. These standards should be regarded as the norm for Christian young people.

F   The Church should do all actively to encourage (and not discourage) all those in cohabiting unions publicly to affirm their marital relationship by undergoing a ceremony of marriage whether in a church or a register office. If the law were reformed to allow the registration of common law marriages, such registration should also be encouraged by the Church.